REFLECTIONS OF
A Chicago
Black Man

POETRY AND PROSE
FOR DISCUSSION
AND DEBATE

I0156815

Arthur Brown Morrison

Copyright © 2021 by Arthur Brown Morrison All rights reserved.

No part of this publication may be reproduced, stored in a retrieval system, or transmitted in any form or by any means, electronic, mechanical, photocopying, recording, scanning, or otherwise, without the prior written permission of the author.

REFLECTIONS OF A CHICAGO BLACK MAN
Poetry and Prose for Discussion and Debate

ISBN: 978-1-943343-25-6

Arthur Brown Morrison

Printed in the United States of America
Destined To Publish | 773-783-2981
www.destinedtopublish.com

TABLE OF CONTENTS

Chapter 3: Affirmation

Chapter 4: Photography as Expression

PREFACE

Poetry! A lot of people prefer not to go there. If it's got to happen, make it a rap, spoken word or lyrics in a song. The poems in this book are for you to parse, devour, analyze, debate, disagree, enjoy or inspire your determination to write your own poetic expressions. You may choose to write just for yourself or for others.

In her book "How to Eat a Poem," Eve Merriam advises about writing, "...don't be polite, bite in..." Another writer says that poems are to be savored because they are rich in meaning.

The poems in this book are intended to represent a composite of male voices and perspectives. They came about in response to a specific challenge: Where is the true voice of the Black male? And, if you're not hearing it, maybe you should write about it.

This challenge came, more than two decades ago, from a sister-in-law, a professor, herself a poet extraordinaire who spent a lifetime encouraging others to write poems or tell their own stories. She published "The Otherwise Room." It is a collection of poems written by friends, family, and acquaintances. She was also a co-founder of The Poetry Factory. You can see some of her poetry at the website www.mariamootry.com for Maria's Poetry Factory Revisited.

In 1995, during a visit to her sister's and while enjoying a cup of coffee with a slice of homemade pound cake, she gladly joined the lively discussion about how African American males are portrayed in popular media. There was a lot of back and forth, heated, yet friendly disagreements. That is when she threw down the gauntlet.

Not one to back down, the author, an engineer by training and whose usual interest favored mechanical things, took the challenge and embarked on a journey he'd never before attempted. The result is this collection of poetry and prose. "Be sure to publish," the professor advised.

BIOGRAPHICAL
SKETCH AND DEDICATION

The author was born in Chicago, Illinois on the Southside. He attended two Chicago public elementary schools. He is a graduate of a Chicago public high school and two colleges. He works at a job full time and continues to investigate and write about life's mysteries.

> To all the brothers
> Who wanted to,
> But didn't
> Get a chance
> For dreams deferred
>   of wisdom lost
> For efforts
>   to thwart despair.

...and in memory to Maria, Professor Extraordinaire

CHAPTER 1:

REFLECTIONS

WRITERS

We writers have no thoughts of our own,
We just travel on other people's dreams.
We listen, we absorb, we make it our own.
We write characterization.
We bring thought to life.

We verb it.
We adjective it.
We subject it.
And we noun and pronoun it.
We describe it.
We dissect it.
Push it, pull it.
Roll it over, roll it under.
And just plain beat it to death. We take artistic license.
We upset and offend.

Throw a punch, or take a punch,
It's very foreign to us.

We believe the pen, is mightier than the sword.
And pretty much that is true, but build a skyscraper
Or span a river with a bridge, it just won't do.

But if you're like me, and would rather discuss
Than trade a blow or two,
Drop your letters, on a piece of paper
And let's see what comes out of you.

BLUES

I got the blues, what's the blues?
The blues is the boss on your back.
The blues is the bill, that won't go away.

The sun is shining, I still got the blues
It's the inevitable answer that's wrong.
The cake that won't rise.
The car that won't go fast.
The hole in your heart.
The flat spot in your emotions, blues.
The itch you can't scratch.
The hole you can't get out of.

I got the blues, my partner in crime.
My cell of gloom, my prison of pain.
I got the blues and they won't go away.

THE HOOD

A brother went to the hood today, to seek what he lost.
That ingredient of life's recipe, something he'd misplaced.
For he'd found success many years ago.
But the success was not of happiness.
His heart was empty, and his body was a shell.
He'd lost his reason for living, his life had gone to hell.

What he'd found, was the place was not quite the same.
He'd felt like a stranger, in a foreign land.
Where there was grass and trees, was now dirt and trash.
The doors were locked, and fear was evident.
Gray gloom had set in, and the sun was cold and mean.
He saw desolation of spirit, of weakened moral fortitude.
And knew that his reason for living was not only for his own good.

For what is wealth, if not shared with the poor?
What is knowledge, if hidden in the dark?
And what is a man, if he turns his back on others?

A brother went back to the hood today.
And that brother was me.

11/20/95

WAITING

One has heard a great deal of clamor about Waiting To Exhale, the book, the movie. Women say, this is their life, men say it's male bashing. Women try to relate or say they can relate to one or more of the characters, men don't want to relate at all.

The book, the movie, deal with four women and their successes and failures with men. One is going through a divorce, another is trying to raise a son, still another is floating between three different men, and finally one is hoping that another man will leave his wife. The point is not that the male community is taking a beating, but more that the women are having a rough time with choices they've made. You must wonder how many men did these women reject to get to these "winners" which they chose.

Are there not more important issues to be dealt with, the state of the community as a whole: drugs in the hood, violence is up, car-jackings are becoming common place. When was the last time you could leave your doors unlocked, and the club is not a place to workout or a gym to shoot hoops. What about the national deficit or more importantly the systematic elimination of affirmative action programs.

To the man I say it's just a small piece of cloth in a patchwork quilt of the media. And as a male, if I'm not satisfied with the images out there, let me write my own books, make my own movies. And if, what the book or the movie says, is true, then we have none but ourselves to blame, if not don't sweat it.

It's fiction, not real, not based on one person's life, but drawn up and diagramed in the author's mind. Oh I'm sure it's happened in someones' life. But ladies it's just entertainment, nothing more nothing less, an escape for a few hours. No prince will ride up on a white horse, or should I say a white Beemer, wearing a designer suit, with a guaranteed prestigious job, smelling good. It's a myth, a stereotype. If you believe everything on the television or at the movies, you may just miss that diamond in the rough. There are good men out there with good hearts, great personalities, who have been rejected, for lack of a six figured salary, no Beemer, average looks, and no designer clothes. Good men just waiting.

DISCUSSION:

According to James Baldwin: "Not everything that is faced can be changed, but nothing can be changed until it is faced." There was much discussion around "Waiting" which was written more than twenty years ago when the author was first invited to try his hand at writing in order to express an African American male point of view. Questions were asked such as "how has the author's point of view changed" or "have cultural values changed over the years?"

After reading the selection, one young man made the comment that he felt that women were setting standards for themselves. "Isn't that a good thing?" he asked sounding a bit exasperated.

An older guy said that he recalled the 1992 novel by Terry McMillan as well as when the 1995 film with the same name was released. He shared how he'd heard a lot of grumbling on the part of his male babyboomer friends about how the Black man was portrayed.

The young man, a millennial, would've been only about nine years old when the film was released. He and his peers exist in a world where attitudes have shifted and women have expectations which they may not have seen as possible twenty-five years ago.

COFFEE

Coffee is like life.
Some like to mix it with water, milk, sugar
But for me, I like it black, with all the caffeine I can have.

Some like to grind and brew their own
Others prefer to buy it, and take it home.
But for me, got to have that morning fix.
Got to have that black gold to go.

Coffee, sometimes smooth, mellow, earthy, full bodied, rich.
Other times, rough, hard, strong, gritty, mean.
But there's nothing like that aroma, to jump start a body.
To open your eyes, and cause the sun to rise on one's day.

And like life: to know a good cup of coffee,
You got to have a bad one now and then.
But, for those of us who need an alternative,
There's always tea if you know what I mean.

CUP OF FRIENDSHIP

Today I shared a cup of friendship with a friend.
We gathered at a hole-in-the-wall bar.
Knocked down a couple of beers.

In the corner, the jukebox played Smokey, Four Tops, and
  Marvin too.
Every now and again, a song brought back a memory,
  hard and true, retracing an old groove in a 45.
Filtered through a smoke filled past, memories as wavy as
  a cigarette's smoky tail.

We talked of hopes.
We talked of aspirations.
We talked of fears and pains.
And of acquaintances we held dear.
Miss Brickhouse has three kids and no more a brickhouse,
but has a condo or two.

Mr. Afro who had the pretty hair the girls love to run thru,
is Mr. Clean if you know what I mean.
We were the same, but life had left its mark on us.

Cuts of pain, age lines of stress, and gray hairs of wisdom.
All formed to paint a picture of time on life's canvas.

And when it was through and we parted to go, we said
we'd have to do it again.
Today I shared a cup of friendship with a friend.

11/11/95

CHAPTER 2:

POEMS OF SADNESS, REGRET, OR SORROW

STAYED TOO LONG

The conversation was lovely, the talk was dear.
I experienced mixed emotions, it played sweetly on my
 ear.

We discussed the world's affairs, solved all its problems.
Reduced crime, balanced the budget, and cut taxes.
Talked about problems between the sexes.
And disagreements between the races.

As we conversed, I wanted to stay.
But suddenly, the feeling smarts,
And It's not in my heart
Now I've lost the conversation art.
I think I stayed too long.

Your company was lovely, your beauty divine.
I have overstayed my due, overspent my time.
And now we can't agree; I would just like to leave.
For my time has rotted like fruit on a dead vine.

I think I stayed too long.

11/26/95

HOMELESS

I am the man on the street
The restless soul who will not sleep
I ask for pennies nickels and dimes
And people flee
But ask me my story and I'll tell you the truth
For I was once just like you
I was a doctor, a lawyer, an engineer, too
I chased a dream of success
And hit life's patches
Greased with alcohol and dope
Got too deep and replete
Now I roam these streets
No place to go or plans to keep
Just trying to stay warm
My house is a shack or shanty
  a cardboard box
Under a viaduct.

VICTIMS

I read an interesting statistic, some say one out of every three black males between 20 and 29 years old will come in contact with this country's judicial system. What does this mean? Well it means something is wrong. Most of the individuals are in for some sort of violent crime against society, and very few are in for white collar infractions.

We talk of black males being victims of society, and moreover the cards being stacked against them. High death rates, from childhood to early manhood, high unemployment, and low educational skills.

Also what of the other victims; innocent citizens who are just trying to do the right thing: those of us who had our cars stolen, been mugged, raped, shot, and various other undeserved experiences courtesy of criminal choices. Likewise what about our loved ones who live in constant fear.

I had a gentleman once ask, how to solve the overcrowding problem in our jails. My response was to lock-up all the law-abiding citizens and let the criminals out. After a few months the system would cease to be overcrowded. Just kidding. On a serious note, there are several victims in any crime; the actual victim or the person to whom or on whom the crime was committed. Also the criminal, who is branded for life. Besides, what about we as black males who are stereotyped? Try to catch a cab, or go into a department store and have security follow you around. Likewise, how about our young men being labeled, as gang-bangers just because they have that look or dress a certain way. Crime makes us all victims, it reduces our basic freedoms, it makes our communities unstable, and rips the very fabric of our neighborhoods.

This is a call to our males to make a difference. We can't become substance addicted, if we don't sniff it, shoot it, or drink it. Men isn't it time to take some of our young brothers under wing and give support, knowledge, and understanding? Furthermore, stop ripping off your brothers, because if the truth be known, they have less than what you've got. And to those of us who claim to be leaders, it's time to show some leadership by not just speaking the golden rule, but living it. Until we as a people show love for one another, the world will show no love for us.

STILL

Though you treat me badly, I am still a man.
Though you neglect me,
I am still a man.
Though you ignore me,
I am still a man.
Though you push me away,
I am still a man.
Though you would have me homeless,
I am still a man.
Though you break up my family,
I am still a man.
Though you promote my woman over me,
I am still a man.
Though you push me against a glass ceiling,
I am still a man.
Though you would pump me full of drugs and alcohol,
I am still a man.
Though you imprison me,
I am still a man.
Though you killed me when I was young,
I am still a man.

Though you cover a rose in manure,
Are not its properties still pure.
Though you label as mere lead, gold;
Does not its value still hold.

Yes, God made me, and though you try to do me,
I am still a man.

11/12/95

I WILL

Will I be worthy, O Lord to be,
Considered a faithful son of thee?

Will I be worthy, O Lord, of grace,
Even though you gave your son in my place?

Will I be faithful, found and true,
Or just another soul passing thru?

Will I be worthy, to run this race,
Or flee, when the world quickens its pace?

Will I be worthy of wisdom given,
Or waste it away, on unfruitful living.

Will I be understanding, of those with less,
Or turn my back, and think I'm best.

Will I be worthy, O Lord and see,
That I am weak and in need of thee?

WOKE IN ANGER

This morning I woke in anger, in search of my very soul.
This morning I went to D.C., maybe not in presence but in
   spirit.
To find my soul, my reason for existence.
To remove these burdens that weaken.
And loosen the shackles that bound me.

What I found were others in search of thought and reason.
What I found were doctors, lawyers, carpenters, men from
   all walks of life.
What we found was responsibility, a call to make a
   difference.
To change the course of our lives, and to give a legacy of
   peace and hope to all who follow in stead.

It mattered not who I was,
Nor caused me to be weak
It forged and annealed my very soul,
Even made me dream:
I am a man
Though you judge me harshly

My strength comes from within.

What I felt was love.
What I felt was peace.
What I felt was joy.
What I felt was a common thread;
That we were brothers beneath.

So after all the high fives.
After all the handshakes,
God grant us grace and vision
to do and tread
where we've never, never been.
I awoke in anger this morning,
Lord, let this not be a wasted emotion,
But a wake up call, forever.

11/6/95

THE MAN

The man speaks, and the world listens.
He does not teach, nor does he protect.
He is not a doctor, a lawyer or engineer.
Thousands come to see him play.

He shoots the ball, three points.
He hits the ball, home run.
He catches the ball, you're out.
He throws the ball, touchdown.
His talents, God given.

He is a role model, as role models go.
But why he should be followed, few really know.
He is imperfect and flawed like you and I.
But is worshipped like a god, and why?

The world stops, when he plays.
Where's the importance; is it just a game?
On the field or the court, he is unequalled
Disciplined, physically strong

Kids want to wear his shoes, his jersey, his team colors.
Even when some can't afford to eat, nor have shelter to
sleep.
Yet, they'd save that last penny, 'cause they want to be
like him.
Read or write well, maybe they can't, and math?... not
taken seriously.

They dream. If they practice, practice, they will make it big.
And have shoes like Nike, Reebok, or Converse, named for
them.
In reality, if they deal with the odds, their chance, seems
infinity to one
That they will remain poor; but still they come.

In this world of abused children
With all the money that changes hands
How about a nickel or two for the kids
And as for being like the man we love,
Hey man, how about giving us some love.

The inscription on a work of art by Paul Gauguin reads "D'ou venons-nous, Que sommes-nous, Ou allons.-nous." Where do we come from? What are we? Where are we going? The viewer is compelled to reflect on these weighty questions. Similarly, a poem can inspire a moment of reflection, of wondering, of questioning about our purpose. "The Man" written more than two decades ago provoked much hearty discussion and debate.

During one discussion someone argued that more should be said about not just the talent but the hard work and indomitable spirit that the athlete must have. The same person mentioned that in a Time Magazine article, a writer points out how our culture fails to label as genius what some athletes are able to do.

Another person pointed out that it was necessary to take into account when the selection was written. The tradition, until fairly recently, was for team owners to put some distance between the players and their old neighborhoods, which in many cases were called ghettos. The kids left behind in the hood were deprived of the opportunity to see what the real life of the athlete was like.

Also, at the time there was a lot of discussion about how school children were underperforming, dropping out of school, and showing less interest in applying to college. As one way to change this dynamic, many schools created career day programs to provide an incentive for students to adopt the idea that: "if you believe it, you can achieve it."

Ironically, a regularly occurring phenomenon was that of a career day guest who would ask a class of seventh graders what they wanted to be when they grew up and invariably the answer was the name of a favorite athlete or popular singer. There seemed to be only a vague idea about how these stars achieve their status and only a minimal awareness of the many other important careers that are vital to having a society that functions well.

Another person pointed out that the selection was written more than 20 years ago. Things are changing. Now, more students are enjoying sports in perspective and have a broader horizon of possibilities from which to choose when setting their own goals.

Technology has contributed to the change. Also, an increased opportunity to learn about how genius combined with work ethic makes the exceptional athlete possible. Recently, during another discussion about "The Man" someone shared an article found at cnbc.com by Tom Huddleston, Jr. titled "How Michael Jordan Became Great: 'Nobody will ever work as hard as I work.' Michael Jordan explains his work ethic and the obstacles he has had to overcome. Such an informative article is helpful when, as one quite young person commented, "people don't want to be like the man, they want to be the man."

The author's daughter offered this: I think super athletes today are far more sharing about how hard they work. I believe Kobe Bryant was renowned for his work ethic and he shared what it took. I think generally the culture has moved psychologically and technologically toward more sharing and that has helped ground notions of athletes being superhuman and not needing to work hard too. Twenty-five years ago, there weren't as many direct mediums for celebrities to interact with their fan bases like there are today.

SEE AND HEAR

O you with eyes and ears
But cannot see nor hear.
For you talk with feigned wisdom,
But lack of common sense.

You claim to be educated, with many degrees,
An educated fool is what some see
You claim to know it all,
Yet cannot see the doughnut for the hole.

You talk of numerous great structures to build,
But talk and more talk is all you yield.
You, who pontificates of greatness,
But never seem to find it.

You seek to network with whom,
But network with what is more like you.
If you would choose to use
those fundamental senses
You'd see and hear clearly the things you'd lose.

AMERICA

America, America, the land that fell on me.
You took me from my homeland and forced me to my
knees.
You enslaved me, you broke me, and called me savage to
my face.

For 400 years I lay destitute and lost in shame.
You stripped me of my cultures, you ripped my soul bare.
You used me, you demeaned me, and left me without a
prayer.

You said it was a crime for me to read, a sin for me to
think.
Declared me less than human, cattle for someone else to
keep.

And still I fought in every war you had to make you strong.
I went away to liberate though you did me wrong.
And when I came home, and wanted to be proud.
You pushed me away and said boy, get down.

And now when they play the National Anthem, I still stand
and salute.
For I too am American, for I have paid my dues.

America, America, must you take all that I have.
What I want from you is simply to be fair.
Follow your creed, for the freedoms of which you speak,
and practice what you preach.

Debate:

What are we? Where are we going? And, a popular question asked in recent times is: "Have things changed?" The debate goes on. The beauty of the written language is that it provides a record. It can give us a reference point on which we can base our arguments.

The poem "America" does this. During discussion and debate one person argued that some things had changed and we should keep working towards more change in the direction of a better world. Another person pointed out that it was important to remember that the poem did not represent a single voice, but a POV derived from many sources such as books, articles, and conversations. One person argued that the author was entitled to "tell it like it is" as perceived at the time.

MY LIFE

This is my life, get your own.
This is my pain, get your own.
My mother raised me, my father taught me.
So get your own.

This is my train, for I bought the tickets.
These are my tracks, for I am the engineer.
This train runs in my direction.
You either ride or get off.
Move or get run over.

This is my life, get your own canvas.
This is my life, get your own brush.
These are my paints, for I paid for them.
And I will make my own brush strokes.

I think what I will, I care not how you label me.
Label me if you dare, face me, but be prepared.
For it is my life and I run it.

CHAPTER 3:
AFFIRMATION

A LOAF OF BREAD

A loaf of bread, a jug of wine,
And thine is what they say.
But for me I'd settle for one,
So long as it's thine, if I may.

For you are my reason for being.
My strength, my power for living.
My beginning and my end.
My alpha and my omega.

For a loaf of bread may feed me,
But it will not forever fill me.
That jug of wine though it tastes fine,
May make me drunk, but not sublime.

That loaf of bread, that jug of wine,
And thine is what is said.
But it's the thee that makes me free,
For I'll go out, and get all three.

THE THOUGHT OF YOU

I love the thought of you in the morning,
It makes my day complete.
It's like sunshine to my soul,
the coffee of my spirit.

Your presence goes by,
Like the smell of biscuits and butter,
Like grits and bacon.
You are the meat of my existence.
The very thought of my reality.

You are that full-course nonfilling meal.
and I love the thought of you in the morning.

THE WOMAN CAN COOK

She ain't much on looks, but Lord can the woman cook.
Fill my plate with greens and fatback, set the table if you're
   able.
Some eat to live, I love to eat.
Cornbread, neckbones, collard greens, smell that aroma
   coming from the kitchen.

Others make the food look good, her food tastes good.
Proof in the puddin', mix those herbs and spices, pure
   magic in the house.
Pots chipped, burnt, dented, old, and scarred, but buried
   treasure deep inside.
Warm, hot, spicy, sweet, pungent, aromas.

Don't skimp on the butter, sugar, or the eggs.
Take me back, when I was a kid.
Give me the cholesterol, load on that fat.
Women forgive me, I mean no disrespect.
But I love a woman who can cook.
And Lord this one can set it out.

Diet today, not a chance.
Run a half a day; tomorrow.
Starve myself, the rest of the week.
But today, I came to eat.

So pile those greens high and wide, throw a big neckbone
on the side.
Cut me a big wedge of cornbread; and grease it real good
with butter inside.

Oh beauty, is a feast to the eyes.
But please my stomach, and the contentment will touch
my soul.

Roll up the block; smell spaghetti and ham-hocks.
Come to the door, chitterlings cooking in the pot.
Got a spoon, got a fork, in those pots, in those pans.
Slap your hands it's ok, 'cause the pleasure is worth the
pain.

Now as I say grace, Lord bless this place.
Bless this time, bless this food.
And bless this woman, cause she sho is fine.
Looks ain't it, 'cause Lord she sho can cook.

Now as I sit here at the table, eyes fill with all the beauty
around
Potato salad, pot roast, yams, dressing, and gravy

And across the table, pound cake, rice pudding, and hot
   juicy apple pie.
So loosen my belt, close my eyes and look out stomach,
   what a pleasant surprise.

And when I can't walk, just lay me by the door to cop a
   nap
For I'm coming back, 'cause seconds and thirds won't do.
But knock a dent in that table, I'm living proof.
'Cause Lord she ain't much on looks, but she sho can cook.

A TRUE FRIEND

You are the song I sing.
You are the word that rings.
In my heart in my soul, in my spirit you are gold.

For though life is gray.
It is always sunny where you stay.
When I am lost, with you I'm found.

You are a true friend.
A soulmate to the end.
When I am weakest and down, you help me to rebound.

Though your beauty is evident.
Your true virtue is from within.
My love for you will never die.
It will always be in my heart and in my mind.

12/05/95

LOVE IS

What is love
Is it something we say to get what we want
Or is it what we feel
When a special someone is needed.

What is love
Does it make us weak. Does it make us responsible.
Does it make a fool of us.
Does it leave us open.
Do we leave our guard down.

And if we fall off the horse
Do we ride again, or just run off forever.

What is love
And how many philosophers have tried to define it;
How many poets have talked about it,
And how many books have been written about it.

And what kinds of love are there:
Love of a husband or a wife,

Love of a father or mother,
Love of a boyfriend or girlfriend
Or love of a sister or brother.

What is love
Philosophers have tried to define it,
Poets have talked about it,
And many books have been written about it.

FINE BROWN THING

Fine brown thing of ebon hue
I want to know can I talk to you
You my thang
I wonder in awe
What moves your mind
Can I call?
While others sit back, stare and fall
I makes my move to watch your back
As you move across the room
Leaving chaos and jaws hanging in your wake
Hold your hand is my desire
Can I carry your books?
Light your fire
Hey fine brown thing
I love you
Big brown eyes
Clear dark skin
Make you mine if I could
Sure would be neat
It be smooth
Be your man, be your friend

Caress your neck, touch your chin
Dance with you
Check out your moves
Just don't want to act a fool
Hey, babe just let me hang with you
Fine brown thing of ebon hue.

64 AT 50

64 at 50 not so long ago
Haunted by phantoms
that won't let go

Ghost tugging hard
Apparitions that won't leave

Still hopes and sorrows past
Hanging on fog of long lost last

What of expected future goals
Just a root of remorse
without a soul

Yet what does experience teach
caught in its web not free to flee

64 at 50 as anyone knows
A worn manuscript
lost long ago

But what is the message
of this meandering ramble
Live for today
   without preamble

Seize the dawn
At its dawning comes the night,
   the night, with nothing calling

You'll wonder
Where 50 has gone
Is 64 plundered,
or pandering on?

A SHOT OF BOURBON

A shot of bourbon
An ounce of sense
Can remove the pain
of lust and remorse
of foolishness spent

To be drunk
and blasted to hell
Or cross-eyed
in a liquored-up spell
Just like when you knew
You should not
   have said yes.
Now here you sit
hunkered over,
Wondering what move comes next.
How do I recover,
Can I flex?

Comes the call, rye,
Bourbon, brandy, cognac or beer.

Some spiritual fortitude
is needed here.

Is an ounce
   of prevention
      worth
         a pound
         of cure.

DEFLECTION

To age well is a timeless excuse
For old men debasing

A collection of old memories a-fading
To remember tales or memoirs of greatness.

To make excuses for wrinkles and crows feet showing
Grey hair or lack thereof not flowing.

Man, I was great and they loved me then.
Now they know me for who or when.

I could burn the candle at both ends
Now like a vampire I hide from the sun,
Like bell bottom pants out of touch.
Tie-dyed clothes faded too much

Here I stand trying
to recapture misspent youth,
Holding on to memories
of liquored clandestine meetings

Lighting a burnt out wick
Of a candle spent long ago
Holding on to a scent,
smoke soot of great adventures past

Reaching for the next beer or stronger
Holding court for others,
lost spirits of candor.

CHAPTER 4:

PHOTOGRAPHY AS EXPRESSION

WHEN THE PHOTO BECOMES THE POEM

Photopoetry? Yes, it's an emerging genre. If you're not already familiar and want to learn more, here's a resource: photopedagogy.com. Each photograph found in this book has a story to tell and can be interpreted as a type of photopoetry.

When the author wanted to learn more about photography, he turned to Chicago's South Side Community Art Center. There he studied the art of taking pictures and explored the skills required to use photographic equipment. It so happens that once technique is mastered, it is the photographer who composes and captures in a click what is sometimes difficult to express verbally. As the adage goes: "A picture is worth a thousand words." So, the photo becomes a poem.

The pictures seen here are of eleven photos with their titles that are associated with poems found in the book. The actual photographs were taken around the time the author took photography classes at the Southside Community Art Center. Included with the titles are locations in Chicago where the photos were taken.

THE HOOD
(WINTER-GARFIELD PARK)

HOMELESS
(NEAR 39TH STREET)

THE THOUGHT OF YOU
(STILL LIFE ON 84TH STREET)

LOVE IS
SISTERS ON SUNDAYS

LOVE IS
A FUN ADVENTURE

LOVE IS
A MOTHER AND CHILD

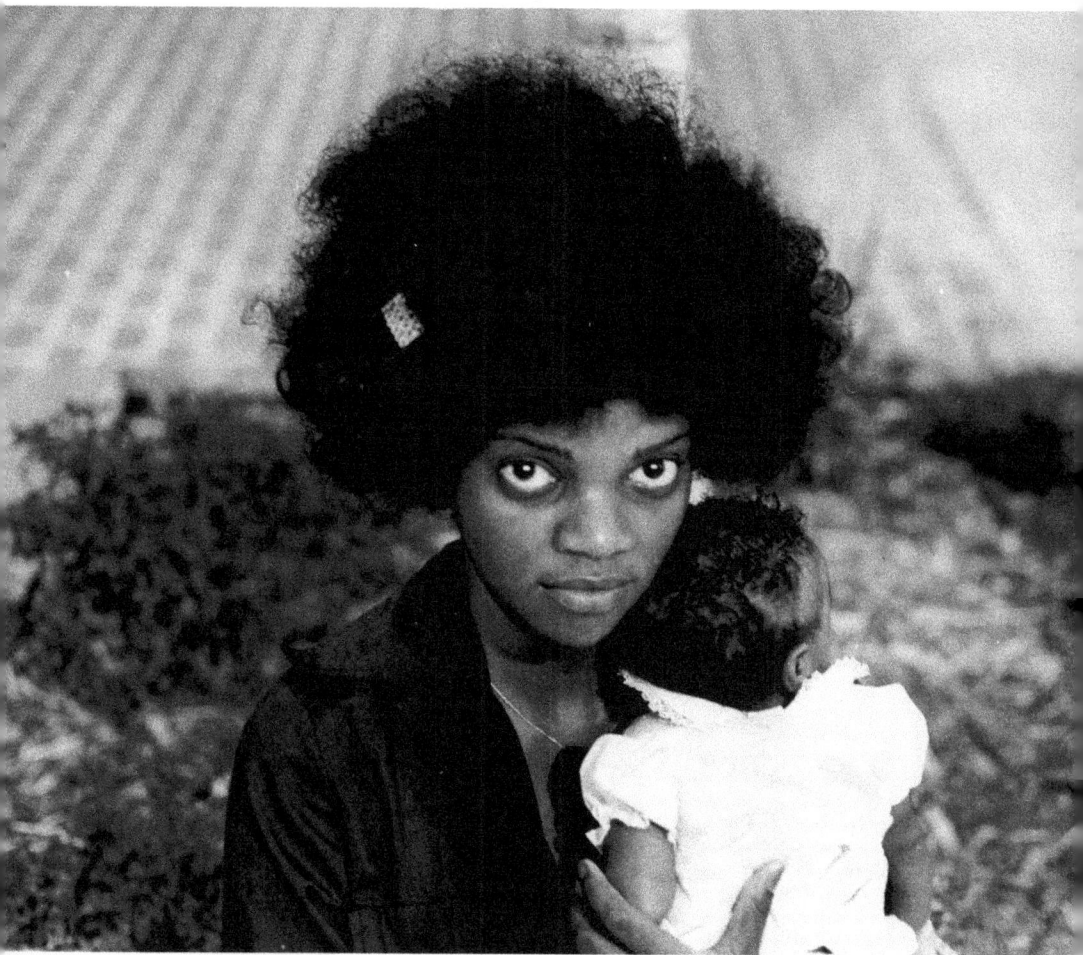

LOVE IS
GRANDPARENTS

LOVE IS
FRAGILE

LOVE
LEAVES MEMORIES

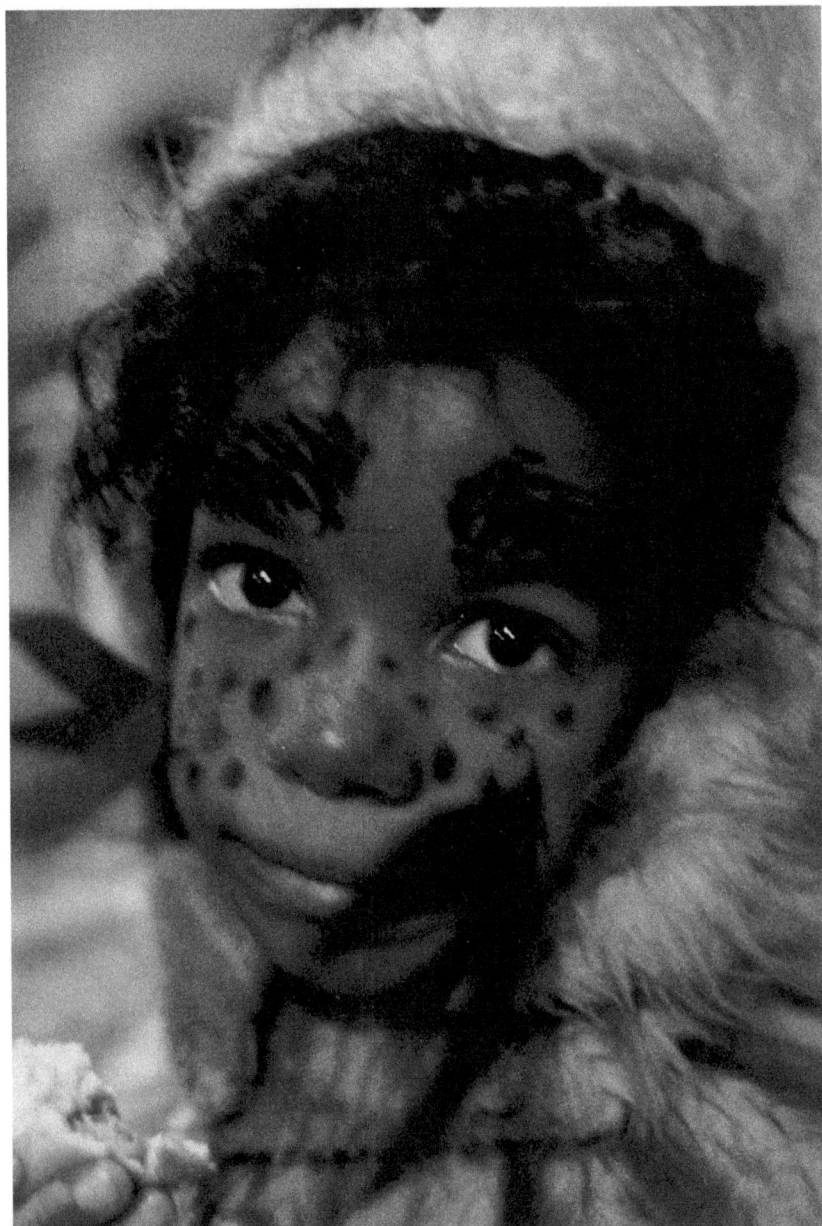

LINEAR THOUGHTS
BIRDS IN A LINE

REFLECTIONS
BIRDS AT NORTH AVENUE BEACH

AFTERWORDS

The author married into a family of writers and poets. His sister-in-law, the professor as he called her, was an authority on the works of Gwendolyn Brooks. They always made sure her popular book, "A Life Distilled: Gwendolyn Brooks, Her Poetry and Fiction" was easily accessible when she came to visit. It was an excellent reference source. In addition to this, several poetry anthologies were always on a small bookshelf in the kitchenette.

The professor often would engage all those present in impromptu recitations either from memory or by reading from one of the anthologies. She'd create a grab bag of slips of paper with titles of poems and names of poets. Each person in the room would be invited to pull one of the folded slips of paper. Then, the fun began. Many poems could be impressively recited from memory. For example, almost everyone in the room knew "If" by Rudyard Kipling, "O Captain My Captain" by Walt Whitman, "I Know Why the Caged Bird Sings" by Maya Angelou and many others.

"What was this all about?" was the author's reflection on the professor's very first visit as he witnessed this improvised poetry fest. Soon, he began to enjoy the camaraderie of this literary game. Nevertheless, the truth is that he still felt a bit left out. It was unfamiliar turf. Even his mother-in-law was a writer and poet. Several of her poems were published in the newsletter of her condo in Chicago's Hyde Park neighborhood. A chapbook of her poetry was also on the bookshelf in the kitchenette and each session almost always included some of her captivating short stories or poetry. She was a celebrity in their circles and was poet laureate of her hometown.

If you could have been there in 1995, when the professor issued her challenge saying, "all who could write, should write," these are some of the poems you might have heard recited, shared, enjoyed, and discussed. Poems that might've inspired the author of this book. They include two popular poems by the author's mother-in-law, Mrs. Helen Rushing and three poems by the professor, Dr. Maria Mootry.

THE CHICAGO THAT I LOVE

The Chicago that I love wears a coat of many colors
    From the fresh green of Spring
        to the lush satisfaction of Summer.

Then comes Fall,
    touting its beauty with an eccentric
    riot of Bushy-ness,
        tainting the leaves from green
        to golden yellow,
        from Red to rustic brown;
        deep tan to sepia/grey.

Now comes the wind,
    stripping the trees of all the crisp, brown,
    aging leaves.
        A river of leaves invading your space,
        and mine with equal abandonment.

Finally, a merciful north wind swoops down
    and carries them away where they'll become a
    part of Mother Earth's never-ending cycle.

The weary trees with their stick-arms,
    bare now, reach toward the Sky,
    and beseech the icy winds of winter

to come and present them with their crowning
glory –
      a Halo of purest snow.

Let rivulets of iced diamonds flow down to the earth
    beneath and settle there in a glistening mound
        to await the brightness of Spring once more

Helen Rushing

LAKE BE A LADY

We've loved you in the Springtime
And all the summer long

Now autumn colors beckon
And still we'll stay our song

Lady, let us love you
As we've done in seasons gone

Tho' stalked by icy winds; snow-peaked and
Tempest driv'n; your ravished beauty, timeless
Turn'd now to winter's stone.

Helen Rushing

DADDY'S WORD-HERITAGE

With LIGHT-HEARTED banter
You saved the day
For how many, WHO CAN SAY?

This is my heritage, my capital:
words that fund the HUMAN SPIRIT.
Liquid, invisible, intangible cash-flow,
Light as air, solid as gold.

Equity for the HUMAN SOUL.

Maria Mootry

IN A DIALOGIC MODE

(Deloria and Friends Talk)

The Lady friends:

"Now Deloria
we know you 37 going on 67
& that sweet sweetback of yours
ain't even 40
but it didn't make no never mind
all of us know you think you fine
& we younger than you
but we wasnt born last night, you know.
What you say
if we say we saw Arleta coming
out your house last night
after you left for the AA meet?
What you say for yourself, girl?"

Deloria's talkback:

"Girl, I got up on this one.
Now lemme tell you
I know you wasnt born last night
& I know that heifer snuck to my house

and said she wanted to fix his hair
 & he let her in, he let that so & so in
my house
but girls, lemme tell you,
I ain't no pushover, you know that
If you act like a rug, you get stomped on
for shure.
But to my mind it's like this:
Honey, just let me tell you,
Deloria just plain too old to kill.
You hear me. Just too old to kill.

Maria Mootry

AT THE KITCHEN TABLE MY AUNT JEAN CONFESSES

Since u asked me, I'll confess. But I AIN'T repentin' tho
Yeah, baby, I love my food.
Smells, like a melody drift into my mind
of sweet corn, buttered...tomatoes, steamed...with okra,
porkchops and peppercorn, brown gravy,
butter dipping mashed potatoes
Hmm-hmmmmm.
And don't forget those greens: collards, mustard, turnips,
sweet with hocks and hot with Louisiana red.
No Ma'am, I aint ashamed.
Smoked ham, sliced in hunks, not thin, honey
Remember that song? "Big fat Mama, meat shaking on
   her bones
Every time she walk by, a skinny woman lose her home."
That's me.
Just kiddin'.
Said I likes food, dont go round stealing other women's
   husbands.

Lemme see: macaroni with cheese, peach cobbler with
    white cream,
cornbread...all with lotsa butter!
I takes my choice: green beans, blackeyed peas!
Pecan pie, chess pie, blueberry pie, blackberry pie.
All with butter, lotsa butta.
Now they say butter's not good for you,
but I say folks gotta live till they die.
If I don't eat what I want, I may not live to be a hundred
    and ten,
but I'll sure feel like it!
Gimme a piece of fresh corn on the cob, Alyce, and put
    lotsa butter on it.
I thank u honey. Lord knows. You's a woman after my own
    heart.

Maria Mootry

The author became accustomed to finding himself surrounded by talk of poetry at least twice a year. Over time, he wasn't at all intimidated. He actually felt intrigued and felt sure that if a person had something to say, that person was qualified to write a poem. He listened as the professor shared poems by Paul Laurence Dunbar and other poets.

She explained how there was a time in the late nineteenth and early twentieth centuries when so-called Negro writers were expected to write stereotypically in a contrived "dialect" if they hoped to get published. You can hear this in the Dunbar poem titled "Little Brown Baby." But Dunbar also wrote witty and erudite poetry such as "The Debt" in standard American English. A collection of his poems can be found at www.poetryfoundation.org.

Everybody in the room always loved to hear the family history stories. The professor would tell how her dad, the author's father-in-law, who was by profession a research scientist with cum laude degrees in physics and chemistry from Fisk University, also loved all kinds of literature. In a voice, reminiscent of Paul Robeson, or James Earl Jones, he would entertain his children with recitations from such diverse writers as William Shakespeare, James Weldon Johnson, Henry Wadsworth Longfellow, Lewis Carroll, Rudyard Kipling, Langston Hughes, Claude McKay and others. There would be lots of laughter and excitement as he would "tickle" them with funny poems and scare them with a poem about the sandman or the boogeyman, saying "Gotcha!" That was enough to both terrify and delight the little listeners.

What a surprise it was, during one of those visits, to learn that the prolific African American inventor, Lewis Howard Latimer, who worked with Thomas Edison and significantly contributed to making the practical use of electricity possible, also wrote and published poetry! One of his memorable poems is "The Ebon Venus." You can find this poem at blackthen.com.

Hearing about Latimer definitely resonated with the author who himself had a degree in electrical engineering. He was in good company. Now, he felt more certain than ever that he, too, could and would write about what he felt needed to be told. He had something to say. He could synthesize some sentiments often shared in conversations with his buddies. It would be called "The Reflections of a Chicago Black Man."

When the book was in its proofreading stage, at one point, the author remarked, "I really miss my sister-in-law." Yes, we all miss the professor. She would be pleased that the book is finally done and is about to be published. We hope readers enjoy it.

www.ingramcontent.com/pod-product-compliance
Lightning Source LLC
Chambersburg PA
CBHW071744090426
42738CB00011B/2554